SUCCESS PRINCIPLES
FOR LEADERS

SUCCESS PRINCIPLES FOR LEADERS

7 STEPS ON HOW TO LEAD WITH LOVE™

GERALD M. CZARNECKI

MILTON RAE
P R E S S

New York

SUCCESS PRINCIPLES FOR LEADERS

7 Steps on How To Lead With Love™

© 2009 Gerry Czarnecki and the Deltennium Group

No part of this publication may be reproduced or transmitted in any form or by any means, mechanical or electronic, including photocopying and recording, or by any information storage and retrieval system, without permission in writing from author or publisher (except by a reviewer, who may quote brief passages and/or show brief video clips in a review).

ISBN: 978-0-9820750-0-5

Published by:

Milton Rae Press
An Imprint of Morgan James Publishing
1225 Franklin Ave. Ste 325
Garden City, NY 11530-1693
Toll Free 800-485-4943
www.MorganJamesPublishing.com

1. Business 2. Motivation 3. Inspirational 4. Self-Help
Lead with Love™ is a trademark of Gerry Czarnecki and the Deltennium Group.

For more information: www.leadwithlove.com

Contents

Mahalo (Thank You) to all of you who have discovered my writings. It is indeed... The Only Leadership Advice You Will Ever need! I wish you the best in success as you Lead with Love™.

Gerald M. Czarnecki

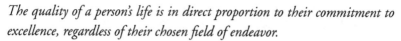

The quality of a person's life is in direct proportion to their commitment to excellence, regardless of their chosen field of endeavor.

Vincent T. Lombardi

INTRODUCTION

WELCOME aspiring **L.E.A.D.E.R.S.**! The foundation of this book is based on my earlier writings of, *You're In Charge… What Now?* The word **L.E.A.D.E.R.S.** is a mnemonic which is intended to aid you in remembering the 7 steps you must take as you Lead with Love™.

This book was written in response to readers like you who communicated to me that they desired further, concrete examples on how L.E.A.D.E.R.S. can apply the 7 Essential Lead with Love™ Principals in everyday life.

Therefore, this book is designed for you and by you. I will provide you with clear and concise TIPS and practical leadership advice, along with an article to support the core concept. I encourage you to refer to this book often, as a ready reference for helping you follow the 7 Success Principles for L.E.A.D.E.R.S. It is my hope that you will not only enjoy but will profit from the thoughts outlined here.

Each chapter is structured identically, in the same reader-friendly format:

Section I — Short Article- Each article will present a topic that we hope will impart useful concepts for you to apply to your work performance. Additionally, it is my hope that it will also encourage responses from you which will generate further thoughts and comments of your own.

Section II — Mini Case Study- This section is designed to help you think through some of the issues that all **L.E.A.D.E.R.S.** must face as they work to achieve peak performance in their groups. I will pose the challenge and then ask you to answer some questions about how you would analyze the situation, and what you might do to deal with the situation at hand. There are almost as many right and wrong answers as there are readers, but I hope that these case studies will prompt you to think about how to practice quality leadership each and every day.

Section III — TIPS from Gerry- This section is designed to offer you practical ideas and guidance that you can take to the work place and implement immediately.

Section IV — "Ask Gerry"- In this Q&A forum, I will answer some of your specific questions about issues that are challenging our readers in the workplace. This space is only as powerful as the questions that are posed to me, so I hope that you view it as an open opportunity for gaining advice or opening discussions about previous issues, comments and/or critiques.

We all get better by learning from each other so please feel free to send me an email at: Gerry@leadwithlove.com. I sincerely look forward to hearing from you and hope that you will not only send me comments and questions, but feedback as well. My goal is simple…I want this to be the most useful resource and tool for your improvement as a leader.

And, for those who have not read my first book, *You're In Charge… What Now?*, I hope that this book will encourage you to get that book so that you can gain deeper insights into the 7 Success Principles that are more thoroughly outlined there.

CHAPTER I

THE 7 PRINCIPLES ON HOW TO LEAD WITH LOVE™

I N my book *You're In Charge...What Now?*, the mnemonic **L.E.A.D.E.R.S.** describes the seven steps to leadership success and each of these letters represents an essential principle for success. While I have simplified the elements of leadership success into seven words, the essence of my message is that being an effective, peak-performance leader is simple, but it is by no means easy. Further, it is imperative that leadership must start with love.

The responsibility of being an effective leader is much more important than being an effective "manager". Every effective manager leads first, and manages second. In my lexicon, there are two things the "person in charge of an organizational unit" does: the first is to lead the people with love; the second is to administer the processes that make up the work. I call this administrative activity the mechanics of managing. These are the activities of planning, organizing, controlling, report writing, etc., and of course the implementation of the technical work of the unit. These are critical activities and can never be ignored, but in my experience those managers who focus the preponderance of their time on the mechanics, ultimately do not succeed. They may achieve short term results, but they usually fail over time.

That which is done "to and for" the people makes a leader a long-term success, not what he or she does to administer the mechanics. Indeed, a manager with great leadership skills can sometimes be successful without being an effective administrator. I have worked for leaders like that, and they were great achievers.

On the other hand, I have worked for leaders who were great administrators but poor leaders, and they were ultimately failures. Simply put: administration may be a necessary condition, but it is not a sufficient condition, for success; whereas, leadership may be a necessary and sufficient condition for success.

My core premise is that if you are to be a successful leader, your success will be determined not by how great an administrator you are, but how great a leader you are day-in-and-day-out. When the staff you are "in charge of" believes that you are a great leader, and when you are taking the seven essential steps as you Lead with Love™, you will become a peak-performance leader who tastes the joy of success!

This book will take you on a journey through the mnemonic **L.E.A.D.E.R.S.** Each letter representing a key leadership principle of how to Lead with Love™:

> **L** for Love
> **E** for Expectations
> **A** for Assignment
> **D** for Development
> **E** for Evaluation
> **R** for Rewards
> **S** for Self

The words are important keys to remembering the concepts, and we will explore in much greater detail how those concepts make a leader effective and capable of being great. I hope that by the time you have been introduced to the seven steps in **L.E.A.D.E.R.S.**, that you will be convinced that leadership is really quite simple, but it will require all of your energy and focus to do well. In short, it's simple- just not easy.

SECTION II — MINI CASE STUDY
"WHO IS THE PROBLEM"

Albert was preoccupied and filled with a sense of unease as he drove to the office. He knew that he was going to have another tough day at work. As the Supervisor of Accounts Payable for the last ten years, Albert was confident that he knew how to do his job, and how to do it right. He could not understand how his new boss, Barbara, who had only been there for one week, could have such a dramatically different view of his job.

Barbara had been preaching to Albert about leading his staff, and about implementing new procedures that, frankly, made no sense to him. Having seen hundreds of people churn through the Accounts Payable Department over the years, he had learned from experience that his job boiled down to one key responsibility: getting the transactions paid on schedule, but not a day earlier than required. He personally processed nearly half of the payments in any given day, while the other three staff members handled the rest. If they got the job done, great…if not…they would be gone quickly.

Paying the vendors was not complicated; therefore, Albert did not see a need to waste time on much more than a quick training of new employees. By focusing on productivity, he had a great record of getting the work out, and he had been praised for years on the quality of his unit's work. In short, he had a great performance record and couldn't imagine why Barbara was complaining. All her talk about management stuff was just a distraction, and had no practical value in Albert's eyes. After all, he has been supervisor for ten years, and has always delivered what was asked of him. How could someone say *after just one week* that he is not doing his job?

As Albert walked in the door of his office building, his anxiety grew. He had barely settled into his desk chair when his boss came in and started the discussion.

Question: Does Albert or Barbara Have The Problem?

Actually they both have a problem...but our limited knowledge of the situation prevents us from determining blame in this case. However, we <u>can</u> identify the signs and symptoms of each participant's problems. Barbara obviously thinks that Albert should do some things differently (or do things that he currently doesn't do at all), but she seems to be in an unreasonable hurry to conclude that Albert is not a good leader. We cannot be certain if her concerns are about managerial mechanics such as reporting, quality control, attendance records, etc., or if her problems are with his leadership activities. In either case, she is certainly being very aggressive, very early.

It is easy to sympathize with Albert's puzzlement about her conclusions after just a week of being in charge. Barbara is probably moving too fast, and has not given herself sufficient time to assess both the performance of the work unit and the performance of the leader. Perhaps her predecessor or her current boss has expressed some dissatisfaction with Albert's performance; nevertheless, she seems to be acting in a highly critical manner very early in the relationship.

I would probably advise her to slow down, listen and observe for a few weeks, and then begin to share her informed judgments with Albert. Her problems with him may be right on target, but she probably needs more time to get to know him and his style in order to determine if he is really falling short of the leadership that she wants.

Albert's own problems are evident in his attitude towards his staff and his job. He clearly is not very interested in helping people succeed, and his singular focus on output may mean that he has huge turnover in his staff. In addition, his thoughts about production suggest that he is doing 50% of his team's output, with three people doing the other 50%. Either he is spectacularly productive, or they are spectacularly unproductive. In either case, this discrepancy in productivity poses a real challenge for Barbara.

Albert's thoughts also indicate that he is not very interested in what we would call either the administrative or the leadership work. He is highly concerned with the bottom line, but his role in leading the staff is a low priority. In the long run, Albert's methods as a "doer" rather than a "leader" could be a serious problem. Our only certainty is that this working relationship is strained after just one week, and unless there is a change of course on both parties, it is in serious trouble. Barbara's own boss will most likely have to take an active role in resolving this situation.

SECTION III
TIPS FROM GERRY

Be Sensitive

When you take on a new job, you should not immediately adopt the notions and biases of the previous boss; it is wiser to make your own conclusions in the first several weeks by doing more listening and watching than speech making. Certainly you need to give some guidance as to your expectations, but you should also be sensitive to the fact that you have now become a "disruptive force" in the lives of your new staff. The change to working for someone new is unsettling and often dramatic. It will take time for them to get to know you…and you to know them. Moving too fast can disorient them, and prevent you from fairly assessing each individual. On the other hand, do not wait for months to pass before making your thoughts known or taking necessary actions. This transition phase is a balancing act, and you need to make certain that the unit's performance is not damaged by one extreme or the other.

SECTION IV
"ASK GERRY"

Rachael: I have a boss who seems to think I'm so good that I don't need any time for the learning process. She keeps piling on projects that are completely new to me, and I feel like she expects me to have them finished the next day. I enjoy the work but I'm totally overloaded, and if it continues like this I won't be able to meet her expectations. How can I tell her to back off?

Gerry: The good news is that you are probably right, and your boss thinks you're great. The bad news is that you really have to be cautious in asking her to back off, because you could damage your ability to be seen as a "star." My first thought is to say, keep trying to keep up. You may be being tested and for now you do not want to cry wolf. Let it go for a couple more weeks, and put in the extra time it takes to get the assignments done, and I might add, done well. The onslaught of new projects may be followed by a quieter period that will allow you and your learning curve to reach a more comfortable balance with the workload.

If the pace does not slow down after a couple of weeks, or worse, if it gets even more demanding, then you will need to talk to her about the problem. Each one of us must decide how much work we can do, and how many extra hours we are willing to put in. If you have hit your limit, and are now passing it, then it is time to have a candid discussion with your boss. The trick will be how you handle the conversation. You do not want your boss to see you as a "whiner", but you need to get your message across. Tell her that you want to do an excellent job, but you simply are running out of time to do a great job. Express your concerns in terms of the quality of the work, rather than the quantity. There is no guarantee that she will react exactly as you want, but if you do not address the issue, you will eventually fail or "burn out". Be sure to let me know how it goes on the first conversation. I'll be anxious to hear!

Matthew: I just started in a new job as a supervisor, and I am already lost. My boss hasn't done anything to help me get started, and the staff is not helping me at all. I have been at this job for about a month now, and I am really worried that I am not getting the job done. What should I do?

Gerry: It is important to recognize that if you are worried about your performance, then there is a pretty good chance that your boss is as well. However, your concern is not a bad thing, as it is a warning that you need to take action. I suggest you do a couple of things: 1) Talk to the former supervisor, if he/she is still around and find out what you can from them. This may not be just your problem. 2) If you have a good friend in management close by, talk to that friend and see if just sharing will get you some insight. 3) Talk to your boss. Now I know that sounds like a really hard thing to do, but you must do it sooner rather than later. I suggest that you ask to see you boss, and in that session <u>ask</u> (not tell) him to advise you on how you are doing and how you might improve. My guess is that if you are concerned, so is he, and this will give him a chance to talk to you about those concerns. You need to do this conversation "yesterday" because the longer you go without the feedback, the more convinced he may become that you cannot do the job.

On the other hand, you may be surprised. Perhaps he thinks that you are doing a great job and you are simply being too hard on yourself. A more likely scenario is that he has not yet noticed the situation, so when you talk to him you will be alerting him to your concerns. With any luck, you will start to get some help. If he thinks that there is a problem with the staff, he may think it is your fault, or he may realize that you inherited some staff problems that need to be addressed. In short, there is much more downside in not talking with your boss. Good luck, and let me know how it worked out.

CHAPTER 2

LOVE

Friends Like But
L.E.A.D.E.R.S. Lead with Love™

HOW many times have you heard an aspiring manager say, "I want to be in management because I like people"? The simple truth is, someone who does not "like people" is better suited to being a recluse than to being a leader of others. On the other hand, I believe that *liking* people can also be a major impediment to being an effective leader.

I suspect that many of you are now questioning my logic, so let me make it even worse. I believe that it is just great for you to like your dearest friends, but you must not *like* your staff, you must *love* them. I have not chosen the word "love" to be inflammatory. I truly mean *love*, not like. The difference between what *I mean*, and what *you may be thinking* is the key.

When I say love, obviously I do not mean erotic love. Nor do I mean the kinds of love that you have for your spouse or significant other or family members. Indeed, those kinds of love are (generally) unconditional.

Some of you know that "Aloha" in Hawaiian means Hello; some of you may also know it means Goodbye; however, it actually means neither of those. Aloha means Love. The Hawaiian culture uses the word "Aloha" to mean a type of love that we can have--and I believe should have--for all of humanity. This Aloha is the love we feel for other humans because they are uniquely human and that they are the most important beings on the planet. This love of people as humans is what I want you to have for your staff. You should love your staff so much that you care for them simply because they are humans and you want the best for them. On a societal level, that may mean the joy of liberty, equality, justice and the pursuit of happiness. In your organization, it should mean that you want them to achieve excellence in their jobs so that your unit achieves peak performance. What is good for their success will also be good for the unit's success.

As a leader, do not *like* your staff. That may seem radical, but it is an essential element of your ability to lead. Liking a staff member may cause you to ignore mistakes made; and by disliking a staff member, you may ignore the things that are done well. Liking or disliking can cause bias in your thinking, and as **L.E.A.D.E.R.S.** we must always remain focused on helping our associates to leverage their strengths and improve their weaknesses. If we cannot eliminate bias, we cannot accomplish that critical goal.

SECTION II — MINI CASE STUDY
"THE FRIENDLY BOSS"

Janet had never been happier in her job than she was two months ago, when she was promoted to Litigation Group Leader in the Chicago office of her law firm. Having been part of the litigation group in the same law firm since graduating from law school ten years ago, Janet was proud to be awarded this new responsibility. It had surprised Janet that the firm's senior partners had chosen her to replace the retiring litigation group leader, as there were several more senior attorneys in the group. Nonetheless, Janet's performance over the years, beginning with working for the most senior litigator in the firm, to most recently winning a really big product liability case for the firm's largest corporate client, had earned her the promotion.

On the day following the official announcement, Janet was proud to receive a congratulations card signed by all five litigation partners in the office. They were all delighted that she had been appointed the new leader because they all considered her a true friend and colleague. That was a major victory for Janet, since the firm had never had such a young partner as a litigation group leader. In short, she had built a warm and comfortable relationship with the other attorneys and it showed in the warmth of their feedback.

That was two months ago. Today was a different matter. Janet was not looking forward to going into work this morning. The firm's managing partner has scheduled a meeting with her to discuss the recent problems in the litigation group. In the last two months, one of the partners in the section (who also happened to be Janet's best friend) had lost two big cases that everybody thought were "slam dunks to win." In addition, two of the best and brightest young associate attorneys had left to join a rival firm in Chicago. She knew that today's meeting was going to be unpleasant at best. Worse still, Janet felt as though her relationships with the partners had deteriorated. They were still good friends, but she was frustrated by the fact that their performances weren't meeting expectations. Although she had not asked them directly, she also had the feeling that they were not responding to her guidance and counsel.

Question: What Caused Janet's Decline?

It is clear that Janet has developed a close, friendly relationship with her fellow attorneys. They all like her and she likes them. In addition, she and her partners believe that those relationships will work to everyone's advantage as Janet takes on her new role as group leader. It is clear that Janet is an excellent attorney who had proven her skills in the courtroom. But, what is *not* clear is why the litigation group has suffered from problems in the two months since Janet took over as leader. There is either a huge "run of bad luck" or there is a leadership problem. Unfortunately, I think we all suspect that it is a leadership problem. My guess is that Janet has made the "liking" mistake.

Leading in a partnership environment is not "slam dunk" easy. Many partnership leaders have been challenged by the "I am your partner, not your subordinate" comment from their colleagues. This factor can pose a real challenge, which seems to be the case for Janet. Indeed, the fact that she has not "asked them directly" about the problems indicates that she is a bit intimidated or uncomfortable with being in a position of authority over her colleagues, many of whom are older than she, and all of whom she considers friends.

The most probable reason for the litigation group's recent problems is that Janet *likes* her associates too much, but she has not yet learned how to *love* them and Lead with Love™. She needs to take her leadership role as seriously as she does her "lawyer" role. She needs to forget that her colleagues are also her friends, and from this point forward, love them enough to have that difficult conversation that addresses her concerns about their performance. Loving them includes dealing with their weaknesses and mistakes. If Janet fails to embrace her leadership responsibilities, her colleagues will continue to see her as a friend rather than a leader. The role of "first among equals" is a challenge that can only be handled if you love your associates, and show it, by being the leader.

In regards to the young associates who quit, their departure may indicate that Janet has a staff problem. She needs to find out their reasons for leaving. It is possible that they really could not learn from the partners, or that Janet's leadership was too weak for them to grow and achieve success. She needs to love the associates enough to make certain that they get the guidance and development they need to become effective lawyers.

SECTION III
TIPS FROM GERRY

If you are promoted to a Leadership capacity, what should you do to start the job? This is a simple question, but there are no simple answers, as it really does depend on the circumstances under which you are appointed. However, there are a few thoughts that you should keep in mind each time you take a new job as you demonstrate that you are committed to being a leader who leads with love:

1) **Interview each person in the group** — Even if you already know everyone, take the time to establish a relationship with each member that says, "You are important to me and the unit, and I want to take the time to focus on only you." This also gives them a chance to tell you what is on their minds. You may be surprised by what you hear.

2) **Stop and Listen** — Take your time, even if you have been there for years and think you know what needs to be done. It's worthwhile to take a figurative step back to look at the unit's activities from your new perspective. Taking the time to observe and listen will pay huge dividends in not only what you do, but how well you do.

3) **Take clear, decisive and thoughtful action** — Do not wait too long to take actions; and when you do, the first decisions you make should be ones that you are highly confident are correct and will be accepted well by the team. This will send a clear signal to them that you can make sound decisions and will avoid having them second-guess you from the start.

4) **Remember what your job is** — For most of you as a Manager or supervisor, you are still a worker, but with the added responsibility of a leader. Do not let the team think that by

being a leader you are going to slack off in your contribution, but at the same time, make certain that you show them that you know that you are now the leader and that they can look to you for that being something new you will do. Remember, you are leading people and that means you need to focus on them more than the work.

SECTION IV
"ASK GERRY"

Katherine: I was just appointed project manager of an information technology project in the IT department of a large corporation and two days into the job, I have discovered that my best friend in the group is the sole reason why our project is being held up. I have known him for ten years, and have worked side by side with him for the last five years and he is truly a great friend! I just cannot bring myself to tell him he is the problem... what can I do?

Gerry: Well, I have a simple question for you...Do you really want to want to be a Project Manager? If you do, then you must get over the "I cannot talk to him" mindset. You either need to talk to him, or you need to step down and resign from the leadership position...I am afraid those are your only two options.

I am assuming that your assessment that he is holding back the entire project is accurate. If so, then you have an obligation to love all of the other associates on the team, and to love your long time friend enough, to face the facts and to deal with it. His failure is hurting the other associates on the team, hurting him and hurting you and your attempt to achieve the mission of the team. Liking your friend is getting in the way of loving him. Remember, your first step as a leader is to Lead with Love™. You need to think through tonight the discussion you will have, and then first thing tomorrow you need to have a conversation with him that clearly, but sensitively, communicates to him his failing.

Bill: Last night at dinner with one of my associates, she asked me to give her two days off. The problem is that we are faced with a huge and critical deadline and I really cannot let her go. She pleaded with me and threatened to quit if I did not let her go. What can I do?

Gerry: I must admit, my first reaction would be...Ok, quit! Now, I know that's not what you wanted to hear, and it is probably not what I would say, but your associate cannot be allowed to threaten you. You need to sit back down with her and tell her that you would be happy to consider the days off at a later time, but unless it is an emergency, you just can let her go right now. In addition, you need to tell her that if she does not understand the sense of urgency, you would be happy to explain it again. As a closing comment, I think it is essential that you tell her that threats are not an effective way to maintain or build a quality relationship.

By the way...I hope that having dinner with her had something to do with work, otherwise, you need to be certain that you are not building a "like" relationship that might get in the way of being a quality leader.

Robert: I have been with my current employer for the past 5 months. During that time I have worked to be part of the HR team that is in place and to learn the culture of the organization. There are two women in the Department that, for lack of a better word... dislike me! I have talked to my boss about the issue and I have addressed the issue with the two women. With over 20 very successful years in HR, this is the first time I've met people that acted like they don't want to work with me. What steps should I take to open better communications and to establish trust?

Gerry: I cannot decipher from your question what the hierarchical relationship is with the two women you are working with, but I suspect that they are more like peers than superiors or subordinates. Assuming that is correct, I sympathize with your problem. I also suspect that this HR Department is not a huge one, hence your ability to remain in your current position will require you to resolve the problem.

All of that said, my first advice is to recognize that there is a pretty good chance these folks have worked together for some time and your presence upsets that comfortable balance they have had. It is also possible that you are seen as a threat to their jobs. I suspect that with all your experience, they think that you may become a career blockage for them, or even become their boss.

My suggestion is a great deal easier to make than to take give it more time. These folks may be intentionally trying to make your life miserable, but you are the newcomer and you need to demonstrate, not through your words, but through your actions and performance that you want to be a productive member of the team and that your goal is to be helpful. A simple idea may be to look for a moment when one or both of them appear to need some help and extend yourself to help them, and make certain that they know that you are doing nothing to take credit for that help. My message is, you need to bite your tongue and try to get them to find it to be a good thing that you are there. Keep trying and I suspect that eventually they will get the message that you are not a threat to them and that you really are a nice guy.

This may not be enough, and you may simply have a situation that cannot be corrected, but assuming you want to (or must) stay in that unit, you are probably the one who needs to demonstrate that you want to be a great coworker. Please let us know how all that works.

Chapter 3
EXPECTATIONS
SETTING THE BAR SETS THE TONE

C AN you imagine playing the game of American football, without knowing the rules of the game? From the name, you would assume that the game is primarily about a ball that comes into contact with the foot. If you were sent out on the field without the rules and without ever having watched a game, your expectation might be that you were to kick the ball past all those people and take it to the other end of the field. Well, if you were in Europe, that might be the case, but the game would probably be soccer, which is actually called "football" in French, Spanish, Italian and German.

Sports are often used as metaphors for our experiences, and in this example the metaphor demonstrates that the name of the game can often be misleading. The only way to play the game properly is to know the rules, and to understand the expectations-- which may be that you should somehow get the ball over the goal line, but not by kicking it. Unfortunately, all too often in the world of work, people are put into jobs and are given far too little guidance as to what the expectations are, hence they really do not know what or where the goal is. This is where every leader must start…You must first define what the expectations are for the unit and for every job in the unit. Without expectations, how can your staff know *when* they have achieved success?

The importance of expectations seems obvious, yet far too many leaders do not focus enough attention on this crucial first step in leading. The key to setting expectations is that they must be clear and specific, so that every associate assigned to that job understands them and is held accountable for them. It is impossible to hold your associates accountable if they do not know what is expected of them; it is also impossible to hold them accountable if you have no way of objectively determining if the expectations were achieved. Every expectation must be measurable, which provides you and your unit with an objective assessment of success and failure.

Much has been written about goal setting, and even more has been written about how the goals get established. It is not our objective here to sell one process or another. There are those who believe that goals that are set mutually by the associate and therefore "owned by the associate" are far better than those that are mandated by the boss. Others believe that clarity, understanding and acceptance of the expectations are the essential elements that make for effective goal setting. Whatever the management style or philosophy, it is clear that without expectations being set, your staff will flounder. In that situation, you and your unit's performance will flounder as well. You must, in whatever way works for you and your associates, make certain that every job, and eventually every person in those jobs, clearly have expectations that guide the work.

SECTION II — MINI CASE STUDY
"A SUCCESSFUL FAILURE"

Brian has been a sales representative at an auto parts manufacturer for the past seven years, and has consistently received great performance appraisals from every boss that he has had. Two years ago, Suzanne took over as his boss, and since then Brian has been very uncomfortable in his job. Suzanne has rarely spoken to him on a one-on-one basis, and has seldom checked on what he has been doing on the job. They've only met occasionally, and it's usually at trade shows or at quarterly national sales meetings where they hardly have a chance to talk. Although Suzanne hasn't communicated it to Brian, he is certain that she is unhappy with his work. He just doesn't know why.

Having pleased all of his previous bosses, and having increased his sales each year (this year was no exception!) Brian assumes that Suzanne is also satisfied with his performance. He inquired with some of the other salespeople about their sales numbers and he determined that his own numbers were somewhere in the middle of the pack, certainly not in the lower fifty percent. Given these results, Brain was convinced that he was doing a good job, and that the problem with Suzanne must be some kind of misunderstanding. He tried several times to talk to her about it, but Suzanne was always too busy for a real discussion. All she had said to Brian was that he should continue to do what he was doing, and to make certain he kept sales growing. Most of the time she would add something like, "Let's make certain we get together the next time we are both in the same place at the same time." Unfortunately, the timing never seemed to be right.

From Suzanne's perspective, Brian is one of the old timers who fail to understand that mediocrity is not sufficient for success. She has some really ambitious sales goals, and Brian's numbers are far below what she needs from him if she is to achieve those goals. Suzanne knows that customers really like Brian, and that her predecessor had been very high on his performance, so she is puzzled by the fact that he is falling short for her. She has nothing against him, and would like to sort out what it is that is holding him back, but she just never has the chance to spend any serious time with him. Her own boss expects her to be making calls on all of the major customers, which takes her out of the office over 70% of the time, and the other 30% is almost always spent catching up on sales reports and senior management meetings. Suzanne is very concerned about Brian's sales and she has been talking to her boss about the fact that she needs to hire some new staff who can take over the key accounts that Brian and a few others from his era are handling. She is eager to move out the non-performers, and to build her team with star sales people. It was clear to her that Brain would have to go.

Question: Is Suzanne A Good Leader?

The quick answer is a resounding no, and the reason is simple...If Suzanne had ever set the sales expectations for Brian, he is certainly not aware of them. We cannot be certain, but it seems that Suzanne has done a terrible job of communicating her expectations to Brian. It is also quite clear that unless Brian really has a serious memory deficiency, he is working in a vacuum where he believes he is a success, although admittedly not a star. Suzanne's view is entirely differently, as she sees Brian as a failure. Hence we have a "Successful Failure." There is a complete "disconnect" between Suzanne's expectations and Brian's understanding of them. Obviously, it is the leader's responsibility to ensure that expectations are understood so there is no way to let Suzanne off the hook.

There is another problem in this case, and it is fairly common in sales organizations. The tendency to have a sales force traveling a great deal, and to be geographically disbursed, results in members of sales teams having very little personal or one-on-one contact with their leaders. This situation means that every opportunity for communication must be used to the greatest benefit. Suzanne needs to plan interactions with her team and with each individual, and must also use each incidental meeting to reinforce her expectations of the individuals and the unit. Being close to the customers is admirable, but being invisible to your staff is unacceptable.

SECTION III
TIPS FROM GERRY

It is essential that every leader focus on setting expectations and setting them at a level that is both challenging and reasonable. "Stretch goals" are great for helping organizations achieve peak performance, but if they are so difficult that they become "impossible dreams" in the minds of the staff, they are no longer stretch goals, they are frustration generators. You must work hard to determine what is truly in the realm of possibility. It may be great to have one of those "Big Hairy Audacious Goals" (BHAG) but if they are so audacious that they cannot possibly be achieved, then they will be disregarded. (Note: If you are not familiar with BHAG, I highly recommend that you read the outstanding leadership book *Built to Last: Successful Habits of Visionary Companies* by James C. Collins and Jerry I. Porras.

In determining goals, you should look at the historical data, evaluate what was done in the past and who did it. Choose a few of the stars in your unit and test your ideas on them. If they think that the goal is far too "stretch", then you can be certain that the others will resist even giving it a try. The opinions of the top performers are critical in a unit. The staff is usually aware of the stars, so if you can get them on board many of the others will follow. If you fail to get the support of yours stars, it will kill the effort with the rest of the staff.

Setting the bar at the right level requires creating some "pain." If the staff can coast to victory, then that is what they will do. If they need to push themselves, then the great people will do that and you will find a new standard of performance. Sometimes the expectations will be mandated from above, and if so, you must embrace these goals and communicate them to your staff. When it is your turn to set the expectations, make an honest assessment of what will be a reasonable stretch for your team, and then inform them of the goals.

SECTION IV
"ASK GERRY"

Iris: I have one staff member who refuses to accept the goals of the unit and his share of responsibility in achieving those goals. His argument is that he has been with the company for twenty years, and therefore knows that the goals are unrealistic. I checked with some other departments, and their goals are very similar to ours.

Gerry: If you have seen other departments in the company achieve goals similar to yours, you should feel confident in the expectations that you have set for your unit. In your case, it appears that you have an "old timer" who believes he is better than your staff and in fact, probably better than you as well. You cannot let this continue. There is no doubt that a one-on-one meeting must happen soon.

In that meeting, you need to first listen to the explanations for his behavior. He may actually have some insights that will help you to understand him. He may also show his ignorance on a material piece of information. Whatever the case, you need to then work him through the logic of the goals. Understanding is an essential first step which he needs to take if you are going to get him to accept the expectations. Do not expect that one session will solve the problem. He has been around a long time and his opinions have been formed and cemented into his behavior. It will take time for him to embrace your goals. Be patient, but not weak. Give him time to see the light, but do not let him ignore it forever. Keep talking to him and reinforcing the idea that these goals are yours and his and that they must be met. Make certain that he knows that you really believe in the goals. A leader's confidence is very persuasive. At some point in time, he needs to come across the divide. If that does not happen, then you may need to move him out of the department.

Sam: My boss gave me a new set of goals six months ago, and I don't agree with them. I do not know what to do about it.

Gerry: Well, if in the past six months you have failed to talk to your boss about these goals, you are in big trouble. Although I would have preferred that your boss get a clear acknowledgment that you accepted the goals, it is nevertheless reasonable for your boss to conclude that your lack of feedback was an acceptance of the goals. It sounds like you did not take the goals seriously when they were assigned, and now that you realize that your boss is actually expecting you to make the goals, you have decided to object. If I were your boss, I would be pretty unhappy. Assuming that you are a leader and have other staff members you are responsible for, you have let them down by not dealing with this problem long ago. Your staff is going to get painted with the failure brush right along with you.

All of that said, I have two suggestions: 1) Talk to your boss and tell him that you made a mistake and should have discussed the goals much earlier. Explain your concerns, and then make it clear to your boss that you are going to make every effort to recover the rest of the year and would like his help in doing so. 2) Talk to your staff and work with them to achieve those goals....you owe that to them, your boss and to yourself. Then...next year, speak up if you think that you have been assigned goals which you do not feel you can meet.

John: I have a staff member who never shows up to work on time. I have told her that she needs to work on getting in when she is scheduled but she's not making any improvements! What should I do?

Gerry: Well, depending on how long this has been going on, you might consider giving yourself a lecture about how you have let yourself down as well as the rest of the staff. The way in which you posed the question to me, makes it sound as though this is a chronic problem, and that you are frustrated with it, but you have taken little if any action. Whenever we allow a single staff member to get away with breaking the rules, we are hurting the entire team. If you have allowed this to happen for an extended period of time, you have in essence told that person it is ok to be late. I guarantee you that she will never be punctual, because she has learned that you don't require it. Worse still, you have sent the rest of the staff the message that 1) you do not care about punctuality (hence they will all start showing up late) or 2) there are two standards, one for them and one for the "late one." A double standard, even when it's merely implied as in this case, will cause the "good guys" to get angry with both you and the "late one."

You must immediately change your own behavior and initiate a conversation with that staff member. Be sure to use the previous lesson, and ask that person to explain why she is late. There may be a very logical reason which you need to know. Once you determine the reason, then you need to tell her that from now on, being on time is required and that whatever the reason, you want to help her figure out a way to deal with that reason. That will demonstrate to her that you care, and at the same time it will start the process in establishing new rules. And, furthermore, these will also be Rules that will apply to the entire staff.

CHAPTER 4
ASSIGNMENT
SQUARE PEGS IN ROUND HOLES NEVER FIT!

YOU will notice, as we go through the seven steps in my the book, *You're In Charge...What Now?* there seems to be a sequential nature to these steps. Life, and certainly leadership, is not always linear or sequential, but there is some logic to thinking about the process in something of a sequential manner. There is little doubt in my mind that starting with the Lead with Love™ mind set- is an essential starting point. You probably agree that setting the expectations for the unit and the individual jobs is a logical first step in the journey toward having a productive work unit. The next step we outline, Assignment, is equally logical as the next step in our sequence. Once you decide what needs to be done (Expectations) as a unit leader, you obviously need to determine how it is going to get done and who is going to do it (Assignment).

Assignment is a critical to your goal of being a peak performance leader, because without the proper structure for doing a job and the proper assignment of staff to that job, there is not much that you will be able to accomplish regardless of your efforts and intentions. Your staff members must have the core characteristics that the job requires for success. No amount of training or leading on your part will be able to make a worker succeed in a job where he or she simply does not fit.

When you staff your team in the world of work, you must make clear decisions about what the job requires and what the person will need to do. Then you have to match that set of requirements with the right talent. Selecting the right people will at least give you a fair chance at achieving your goals. Without the right knowledge, skills, attitudes and work experience, your staff will undoubtedly fail.

Choosing the right people for the job is one of the toughest tasks you will be asked to execute as a leader. The recruitment, employment and placement of the right people is both an "art" and a "science." There are many right and wrong ways to go about hiring your staff, but rest assured that success is not guaranteed on every hire. You will make mistakes (just as I have many times over the years) but you should try to learn from your wrong choices in order to improve your ability in hiring. Every wrong hire is far more expensive than the out-of-pocket costs associated with attracting and processing a new hire. The loss is even greater when you consider the cost of turnover when the hire fails.

The key to effective hiring is effective interviewing, and the key to effective interviews is to use your ears and brain, not your mouth and vocal chords. My most important advice to you for interviewing candidates is to listen to *their answers*, not *your questions*. You may ask the right question but still come away with a bad decision if you fail to listen carefully to the response. You must process the answer as a piece of information that you can use to evaluate the capabilities of the candidate. All of that said, interviewing takes practice and a solid understanding of human behavior. If you can get help in the form of formal training, take it. It will probably pay huge dividends for you.

SECTION II — MINI CASE STUDY
"THE WORLD'S SHORTEST INTERVIEW"

Heidi was about to start the interview when it occurred to her that she did not have the candidate's resume. She hurriedly looked through several files, but then had to give up because Kyle had arrived for the interview and was waiting for her in the conference room. Out of time, Heidi went to the conference room to do the interview. "Hello Kyle," Heidi said, as she walked in and extended her hand to shake Kyle's. Kyle muttered a hello, and following the hand shake he sat down as soon as Heidi did.

"Kyle, I've misplaced your resume, do you have a copy?" Heidi asked. Kyle was caught off guard and said, "No, I forgot to bring one." Heidi told him not to worry, that they could proceed without it. "Tell me," she began "why do you want to work here at Dalton's ?" Kyle was a little surprised by the question, but answered, "Well, I use your products and I think that your benefit programs will give me an opportunity to work on a graduate degree. After that, I don't know what I want to do. Are there a lot of opportunities to move up the ladder at Dalton's?"

Heidi was not overly impressed with his answer, but she told him that she understood how difficult it can be to think about the future. "How would you plan to use an advanced degree to further your career?" she asked.

"Well, I am convinced that the people with graduate degrees get the best jobs. I want to get a graduate degree while I'm young so that I can leverage it for that much longer," Kyle replied.

"What are you planning to study in graduate school?" asked Heidi.

"Well, I don't know, but it's not going to be accounting-related. I don't like accounting at all," he said. "I think that I can get an MBA in sales and marketing, which is an area that should be a real advantage for me in the job market. Heidi was now convinced that she knew enough, and would hire Kyle because he was smart, ambitious and immediately available. Filling the job quickly is a priority for Heidi, and she is certain that Kyle has all the tools to be successful. She thanked him and told him she would get back to him the next day.

Question: How would you score: the interview, the Interviewer and the candidate?

Obviously, the interview has been shortened to allow room for this discussion, but honestly, I give it a failing score. Both Heidi and Kyle performed dismally, and the interview was essentially a bust. Her questions led immediately to the subject of graduate school, rather than the critical information about his knowledge, skills, abilities and attitudes. She learned nothing about what Kyle has done or even could do. In light of the fact that she also didn't have his resume at hand, it seems that all Heidi knows about Kyle is that he wants to go to graduate school and study something.

Kyle has learned nothing about the job, and the only thing that he has revealed about himself is that he wants to go to graduate school. His unusually honest admission that he doesn't know what he wants to study is unnerving, because it suggests that he hasn't even thought about it. His negativity about accounting may be a red flag that he can't deal with numbers, which are the bottom line of most companies. In short, neither party performed well nor learned much of anything.

One crucial mistake that Heidi makes shows up at the very end of the case. She obviously has a major hole in her organization and thinks that she must fill it immediately. This is perhaps the biggest mistake that you can make as a leader who is in the Assignment phase of leading. Remember that making a bad hire to just fill a hole is worse than leaving the hole. Never hire a "body" to fill a hole in your organization. It will always be a costly mistake.

SECTION III
TIPS FROM GERRY

The interview can be a great tool or simply a waste of time. It is essential that you manage the interview, and that you get your agenda covered in the time you have. Here are some ideas for a helping ensure a solid interview:

Interview TIPS

1) Leave enough time to learn something substantial about the candidate. A 15 minute interview is going to be useless; allow at least an hour.

2) Make certain that you and the candidate can be comfortable. Neither should want the interview to end quickly just because the chair is uncomfortable.

3) Avoid questions that have a yes or no answer. Structure the questions so that the candidate needs to think and respond with more than one sentence.

4) Ask questions that focus on things that the person has *done*, rather than things that they *might* do. You are trying find out what they can do, not what they think you might want to hear as the "ideal answer."

5) Make certain you give the candidate a chance to ask you questions. You can learn a lot about the candidate from the questions asked.

6) Do not telegraph to the candidate in the first interview that you are going to hire them. You need time to consider the fit, as do they.

7) Get references, and check them. There are constraints on what people can say, but you need to talk to people who know the candidate. Avoid their friends; find bosses.

8) Take notes

9) Listen, Listen and Listen!

SECTION IV

"ASK GERRY"

Gloria: I have 12 people who report to me. One of the 12 has been demoted from an intern down. This person is bitter about the demotion, but he is performing up to standard. Every now and then he expresses his opinion that he is more qualified to be a manager than existing managers. Additionally, he is paranoid. Anytime he receives non favorable reviews or comments about himself, he states that this is a plot to fire him. Anytime something is not what he believes it should be, he wants to grieve the situation. Most of the time his grieving is in vain because he has overlooked important information.

What are your suggestions on managing this type of person?

Gerry: When people get "demoted" they almost always get "demotivated." That is without question what has happened to your associate. Indeed, the paranoid view of the world is pretty predictable. I think if you put yourself into the same situation, it is pretty clear that you would not be a happy camper. In fact, your associate is probably not paranoid; he is probably correct. By that I mean: something serious must have been found in his behavior or performance for him to have been demoted. Assuming it was serious enough to demote, but not serious enough to fire, then he is probably convinced that the next shoe to drop is for him to lose his job.

But all of that does not answer your question. The first thing you need to do, is to be certain that you are behaving in a fair and objective way about his performance. Since I do not know from your question what caused the demotion, I can only assume that you did not cause it to happen and may even have inherited this associate. Whatever caused his demotion, he has now been punished and it is imperative that you treat his work objectively.

On the other hand, he is not making it easy for you to deal with the situation. Although I am assuming you have already talked to him about his behavior, my guess is you have not been very direct. Unless, and until, his performance deteriorates, or he actually has a negative impact on your other staff members, I would suggest you give him time to get thorough the healing process. He has taken a body blow and you need to give him time to get the grieving out of his system. If it does not slow down, or if it gets worse, then you are going to need to take some action.

Obviously, you need to follow your organization's policies and procedures for progressive feedback and documentation, but my suggestion would be to go beyond that. If there is any reason for you to believe that you or your other staff members are being "blamed" for his demotion then he may become an unhealthy element in the group. If he does not eventually seem to be "getting over it", then you need to consider trying to find him another job in your organization where he does not have all the memories and constant reminders of his failure. This guy may be a serious problem to you, but if he can not heal his anger, he will be a serious problem for himself as well.

One last thought, if your organization has an EAP (Employee Assistance Program,) you might want to consider encouraging him to take advantage of some of what the plan has to offer. He clearly needs to get over his anger, so you should try to help him in any way you can...that is until he fails to do his job. Then, you have a duty to your staff to deal with the performance issue.

CHAPTER 5

DEVELOPMENT

THE GOOD GET BETTER, THE BEST EXCEL!

HOW many of you went in to work this morning hoping that today everything would go perfectly? Your staff will be productive… there will be no errors, no complaints from the customers or the boss, and all work will be done on time on budget… there will not be a single personnel problem because the entire staff will be humming as a team. Such days are rare in any work environment, but they can and do happen. "Perfect days" happen when the team members are all working to achieve mutual goals and they are all excellent performers.

Most leaders have never experienced a perfect day. Indeed, many years ago, a cynical but probably all-too accurate friend of mine said that his definition of management was, "…one damn thing after another." I laughed when I first heard that, but every time I have used that expression with groups over the years, I get this knowing nod that clearly suggests that there is painful truth in the comment. Being "In Charge" means being responsible for a sequence of challenges that need resolution. In short, each day is spent going from one problem to another.

What can we do to make the transition from the status quo of endless problems to the productive hum of perfect days? Some would say: nothing. There is no chance to be in the "perfect world" because life is tough and unfair, and every job involves reckoning with reality. Others, and myself included, believe that (although perfection is probably never achievable) striving for perfection is a rational goal. Unfortunately, most of us do not strive for perfection; instead we settle for goals well short of that. A discussion on "striving to be the best" is a subject for another day, when I address continuous improvement as a core value for all **L.E.A.D.E.R.S.** Today's focus is on *helping your staff* constantly strive to be better.

Every leader must be committed to helping their associates grow and improve. This requires a commitment not just to giving your staff the opportunity to achieve, but also to developing their capabilities. As **L.E.A.D.E.R.S.**, we must commit a major part of our normal work day to helping our staff grow. We must teach, coach and support the growth of our associates. Anything less would be neglecting our core leadership responsibility. Development, the center word in our **L.E.A.D.E.R.S.** mnemonic, is the central concept in the journey towards becoming a leader. Everything we have discussed before builds up to Development; everything we discuss after follows on Development.

Developing staff is hard work. If you are developing staff, you are not going to go about your own work and enjoy a day of perfection. You are helping your staff to find mistakes, avoid mistakes or recover from mistakes. Your day can only get better, and come closer to that perfect day, if you are working with your staff to grow and improve. If you want a day where you can enjoy the pleasure of no problems, then you must invest in your staff so that they can develop their knowledge, skills and even attitudes that affect performance. Fail to invest in them and you will fail to reap the rewards of peak performance by your unit.

SECTION II — Mini Case Study
"Leave Me Alone"

Janet was into her third week of work as the new supervisor of an accounts receivable department and she was having a tough time. Fran, her most senior clerk, was simply not responding to the feedback that she had given her last week. Janet had watched the error reports coming in from the system and had found that Fran had the highest reject rate of any one of the processing clerks . In a feedback session last week, Janet told Fran the data she had found and Fran blatantly told her to, "Leave me alone, I have been doing this for seven years and I know what I am doing." Janet didn't know what to say, so she just walked away.

This week, the quality reports from the system indicated that Fran's error and reject rates were even worse. Janet decided that she would talk to her boss about the problem and when she did, her boss told her that Fran has always had high reject rates, but that she always caught up on her backlog. He also added that she was a loyal and reliable employee who had great attendance and had stepped in when he needed help with overtime work. Janet asked her boss if Fran had ever been to the new formal training program on the accounting system and he said no. "In fact," he said, "Fran was asked to go about ten months ago and she refused, saying that she was too busy at the job to take the time off. I agreed with her that she was busy and told her we would work her into another session, but we never did find the time. You probably need to try to find a convenient time to get her to the training."

Janet went back to her desk and remained frustrated. She now knew that she wasn't going to get much support from her boss, other than his agreement that Fran should go to the training.

Question: What Should Janet Do Now?

This is not an uncommon situation, and unfortunately, the attitude expressed by Janet's boss is not unusual either. Janet really has only two choices: 1) Leave Fran alone and hope that she does not get any worse or 2) Work with Fran to help her understand and correct her problem.

Most L.E.A.D.E.R.S. will take the first option, and assume that they are taking the lower-risk course of action. It could be the lower-risk choice for Janet, but that is assuming that she expects to be in this job for a short time, and that her current boss remains her boss during that time. I could not recommend that she follow that path, but we all know how tempting it is.

Option two is really the only correct scenario. It will be a challenge, and it comes with the risks that Fran will complain to Janet's boss at a minimum, and possibly even quit. Despite the risks, Janet must commit to helping develop Fran. It is essential for Fran to attend training; and if Janet can arrange it within the budget, she should eliminate the possibility for excuses by having someone take over Fran's work during the training period. Once she has been through training, it will be much easier for Fran to focus on the process she should be following and to ensure that she is using the system correctly.

There is no fast solution to this problem, especially given the position that Janet's boss has taken. Janet should go slowly, but she must proceed with efforts to help Fran grow. It is as essential for Fran's long-term development as it is for the well-being of the unit.

SECTION III
TIPS FROM GERRY

Train...Train and... Train Again!

There is no easy way to get associates to commit to training unless the leader sets the pattern early. In the preceding case, Janet made the mistake of not acting immediately to get her associate trained. Most

L.E.A.D.E.R.S. have access to training programs for their staff. The smaller organizations may rely on "On the Job Training (OJT)" more than larger companies, but every organization has some process or resources for training new staff members. If you have formal training programs, then you should be firmly committed to sending all of your staff through those programs. You cannot allow the pressure of "getting the work out" serve as an excuse to deny them, you and the unit of the knowledge and skills developed by training. When it's possible, new associates should attend training well before they take on a full work load in the unit. It is much easier to give them up during the time that training requires *before* you have become "addicted" to their output.

SECTION IV
"ASK GERRY"

Paige: I have been the supervisor of my department for two years and I have never been trained. What should I do?

Gerry: It is a sad reality that many supervisors have not been trained in the technical aspects of their job; but the more serious problem is the lack of leadership training. I cannot decipher from your question, but I assume that you have not been trained in either aspect. Therefore, the following is my suggestion for you: Start by asking your boss if they have any training in the organization that would be helpful to you. My guess is that there is training of some type, but that you were not assigned to participate because your boss had the thought "I can't have her go to training because I need her here and there's no one to step in and supervise her section". If you get a response like that from your boss, then I suggest that you go to HR and ask them what training is available. You can then go back to your boss with a request to go to a specific program, and make it easy on him or her by proposing a plan for covering your work unit while you are gone.

If that does not work, then you are going to need to create your own development plan that will enable you to grow on your own. Some activities for you to consider include attending seminars or other courses, finding a mentor, and reading books that will help you to improve and learn. It may not seem fair, but it is essential for you to take responsibility for your own growth. I will talk more about this in an upcoming issue of the newsletter, so stayed tuned!

Jack: I have been working with a really weak associate for more than a year now and I have been trying to boost his performance, but he just isn't responding. I'm wondering what I should do at this point?

Gerry: Make certain that you have tried a variety ways to assist his development. Sometimes we continue teaching or coaching somebody precisely the same way, over and over again, even when they do not get it. I have found that as a teacher or coach, it is essential that I try different approaches because not every one learns in the same way. Try using different examples, different times of the day or perhaps having somebody else do the coaching. It is possible that a new approach will be exactly what your associate needs.

If you can honestly say that you have tried all of the reasonable approaches, and that there is still no improvement, then it may be time to have a counseling session with your associate. Although it's difficult, it may be time to say, "I'm sorry, but I don't think this is the right job for you." You may be very surprised to find that he already knows that, and you are simply voicing his own frustration. If that is the case, then the two of you can work on solving problem. Perhaps he is better suited for another job in your unit, or a different unit in your organization. There are times when you truly cannot help somebody improve. That is not defeat or failure on your part, it is simply reality and you owe it to your associate, yourself and your organization to deal with the mismatch.

Julia: I have a staff member who left the office today without telling me where she was going, and she hasn't come back. It's Friday and I know I need to have him do something on Monday, so what am I to do?

Gerry: Julia, it's probably be too late to help you, but if there are any other readers that have had this happen to you, my advice is…do not wait until Monday! Your employee's behavior indicates a serious problem, and you need to find out what has caused it. There are a great many possible explanations. She may have gotten a call that a family member has just died, in which case, you want to know that so you can offer your support. It could be that she had a huge confrontation with a fellow staff member, who failed to explain to you what happened. In that case, you need to get to the bottom of the conflict for the unit's sake. Perhaps you and she had a confrontation that went over the emotional line that she could handle. You might not even have recognized that you caused the event. In any, in fact in all cases, immediate action is called for. What should you do? My answer is… you need to call her.

CHAPTER 6
EVALUATION
L.E.A.D.E.R.S. SUCCEED BY MAKING JUDGMENTS

WHEN most of us begin our first job, we have been through the process of being schooled and tested for the skills and knowledge that we have gained. Virtually our entire lives, we have been evaluated on our success. We have been in constant competition, whether it was against the standards for an A, or against an opponent on the sports field. People have made judgments about our performances throughout our time in school, and when we entered the work place it only started all over again!

There is no escaping the process of evaluation. Students get grades; workers get performance evaluations. As a leader, you are required to make those evaluations. I suspect that when you gave your first performance evaluation, you realized that all those people who had been evaluating you probably experienced the same emotion you were feeling…anxiety. Yes, every time I do a performance evaluation I feel anxious, even uncomfortable. It is no fun being put in a position where I am the "judge' of someone's performance. I imagine that evaluating your staff makes you uncomfortable as well, even if you're like me and have done it many times over the years.

So why is that? Well, for one, it means that you must have criteria against which to assess the performance (you may recall that these criteria are part of "Expectations"—the first E in **L.E.A.D.E.R.S.**). This poses a problem for the many leaders who never clearly defined and communicated the expectations. How can you make this evaluative judgment if you, and worse still your associates, are not clear on what the expectations were for the period of evaluation?

Even if you had stated the expectations, how do you make a judgment about how well they were met if you do not have effective measurements of performance, let alone a clear evidence of that performance? On top of all that, most of us know that if we give a positive comment, it may not be strong enough to elicit a favorable reaction from the associate; conversely, if we give a negative or unsatisfactory comment, we can almost certainly predict that there will be a disagreement from the associate. In any case, the conversation can end up being an emotional and maybe even confrontational event. Few of us enjoy that type of interaction.

Despite the difficulties, every one of us has done a performance review and somehow gotten through it. Whether the review was effective is a different issue. Far too many performance reviews are so weak on either facts or focus, that they fail in their intended use as a constructive part of the development process. They become either poor report cards, or perhaps even super high grades, which reflect only our unwillingness to deal with conflict. More often than not, evaluations are done once a year and reflect not our judgments about performance and how it can be improved, but rather our judgments and conclusions about performance and how it reflected success or failure. Indeed, performance evaluations done infrequently are simply too little too late.

Every leader must learn that an evaluation should be made frequently enough to be judgmental <u>and</u> developmental. As **L.E.A.D.E.R.S.** we are required to make judgments, but those judgments should start as a developmental effort, not a final judgment and disposition. Yes, we will ultimately need to decide success or failure, but along the way, we must give adequate feedback so that our associates can learn from the critiques. If we do not give that feedback early and often, we are failing our associates. Quite frankly, many people in the working world do not really understand how well they are doing in their jobs, and it is our responsibility to make certain that they do.

You may recall that I said earlier that being a leader is simple, but not easy. That comment is never more accurate than during an evaluation. If you have done a good job of defining expectations, then the criteria for assessment and evaluation are already established and it is quite simple to tally up the achievement and score the performance. That is the simple part; the "not easy" part is actually giving the feedback. Most leaders, and I am no exception, do not find these feedback sessions easy. Unless you have a super star working for you, there is always something that you will say that will be a negative comment. If your experience is like mine, you know that will engender some disagreement from the associate, and most of us do not like the emotional stress of a disagreement. Nevertheless, that conversation is essential for the organization, you and the associate if you are going to improve the performance of your unit. It is not easy to follow through, but we must make these judgments if we are to assure success in our units.

SECTION II — MINI CASE STUDY
"THE ANNUAL REVIEW"

Jackie has been the supervisor of the call center team for just over a year and it is now time for her to give her staff their annual reviews. Three of her weakest- performing associates are up for review and she is truly dreading those sessions. In each case, she is convinced that the employee is not going to make it, but she is just as convinced that not a single one of these employees will agree with her assessment. In fact, they apparently think they are doing a great job, as she heard from another supervisor that each one of the weak-performers is expecting a big raise.

Since the first of the year, Jackie has been keeping elaborate notes about what each person has done; both the good and the bad. There is no doubt in her mind that she has the facts to support her evaluation of each employee. Once the performance appraisals are completed, she can send the documentation to the HR department, and she is certain that they will be very comfortable with the facts and will recommend terminating the employees. In spite of being confident in her assessment, Jackie is nervous and uncomfortable with the prospect of doing these appraisals. Her boss has agreed to her request that he sit in with her, and this afternoon they will do the three annual review sessions together.

Question: What Should Jackie Do?

Quite simply, I think Jackie and her boss should cancel the review sessions and instead have a meeting themselves. Unless we do not know something about the last year, the story suggests that Jackie has never talked to the employees about their performances. If this is the case, then I suspect that if she goes forward with the performance evaluation sessions as planned, these three associates will become "unglued." There is no doubt that if I was working for a full year and believed that I was doing a great job, only to learn at the end of that year that I had failed, I would be more than a little upset. Worse still, Jackie seems to think that she will be able to take these "facts" to the HR department and that they will terminate the employees.

In my experience, most well-managed organizations have a policy that requires a process of feedback about weak or failed performance because it gives employees an opportunity to improve performance over time. I suspect that Jackie's organization is no exception; hence, it is likely that the HR department would tell her that they cannot support her termination request of the employees.

Jackie may not like the idea, but she probably needs to begin the progressive feedback process with these meetings. She should treat these reviews as the first in a series of meetings that will be required to either improve performance or to "build a case" for termination. Any other course of action might possibly be illegal, and at a minimum, would be unfair to the associates.

SECTION III
TIPS FROM GERRY

Deciding when and where to have an evaluation session is worth a few moments of reflection. The key to this decision begins with the assumption that you want the session to be at a time and place that is conducive to the associate accepting your feedback as valid and constructive. This means that you want the associate to be open to your comments, not resistant. Think of these factors:

Evaluation Session Thoughts:

- Is this associate a morning person or an afternoon person? Schedule the session when he or she is most likely to be alert and responsive.
- Reviews tend to make even the great performers feel insecure, so choose a setting that is comfortable for your employees.
- Hold the session in a place where you are not using your "power of authority." If you have an office, don't sit behind the desk. If you don't have an office, try a conference room with a round table.
- Consider the associate's most recent positive performance, and start out the session with a strong comment about that success. This is particularly important if you are going to be giving a lot of negative feedback.
- You should dress in an outfit that does not emphasize your power, but rather is more comfortable. Take into consideration your associates' attire as well, and whether they might feel more at ease on a casual attire day.
- Try to avoid sessions when you know that the associate is having

problems in his/her personal life. That distraction will make it hard for them to be effective listeners.

SECTION IV
"ASK GERRY"

Mary: I just interviewed the best candidate I have ever talked to, but she wants twice the salary I can offer, what should I do?

Gerry: That is a great question. My first response is: I hope it was not the first interview, as I always try to avoid salary discussions during the first interview. Furthermore, why was this a surprise to you or to her? Did your job posting, advertisement, or recruiter clearly communicate the salary range?

Regardless, you need to be very straight, very early on. If we assume you are not the owner of the business, and that there is an HR person or business manager who is setting the salary, then you have probably been given a range that is not going to materially change. The candidate needs to know that the salary range is firmly set, and that you will not be able to pay more. Perhaps this will cause the person to walk away, so you must be certain that the range is indeed firm and non-negotiable. If the range cannot be adjusted higher, then you are most like going to be looking for another candidate.

You should be aware that many people go into interviews with grand ideas. Candidates sometimes ask for the moon and hope that they can compromise on a level that is well in excess of what the employer originally wanted to pay. It is reasonable to assume that your candidate is not firm on the salary that she told you she wants. There is no doubt in my mind that candor on this matter is generally the best policy. You may find that this candidate is "playing a negotiating strategy" and you just need to level with her and say that there are limits to what you can do.

Tony: I interviewed a candidate two days ago, and told him I was going to make a job offer. Now I have found a better candidate. How do I get out of this soup?

Gerry: Well, if you had read this newsletter and the Leader Tips before the interview, you would have known that it is a bad idea to commit to an offer in an interview. But then, you know it now. The best advice I can give you now is…just tell the truth…you have chosen another candidate. It will embarrass you, and your organization, but you want to hire the best person for the job. Assuming that you have not made the first candidate a job offer in writing, you have no obligation to make a formal offer.

Your predicament is a good example of the reason for companies—large and small—to use a written offer letter as a matter of policy. That way you will be able to say that until you have written an offer letter, there is no job offer.

CHAPTER 7

REWARDS

AN ORGANIZATION ELICITS THE
BEHAVIOR IT REWARDS

WHEN did you first learn the word, "No"? You may not remember, but I suspect that you learned it from your parents, and you were probably pretty young as well. In fact, it was probably so early, that most of us have no recollection of the when, but certainly we remember the meaning. This negative word carries great power since many of us learn what "not to do" much earlier than we learn what "to do." Frequently, we also got the message that our parents were unhappy with us, and the result of that was some type of rejection or even punishment. Another kind of negative learning, for example when we touched something that was hot, occurred when we experienced pain along with the "No." It did not take long for us to learn to stay away from the hot object.

Unfortunately, negative learning tends to continue through much of the rest of our lives. Too much of what we learn is the "what not to do" and we are find out "what we should do" by trial and error. We get lucky when something produces a positive result, so we try it again. Enough times and we find a success pattern that we can follow.

Returning to the infant example…when we discovered that by using our arms and legs correctly we could crawl to another location, we perfected that process. Our curiosity was satisfied and we learned a motor skill. When we crawled to our parents, or later walked, we got stroked by them and their praise, excitement, loving touch or even a reward of a cookie or a sweet, gave us a learning that was powerful and fun. We probably then did it over and over again and before long, we would be walking and eventually talking.

Ironically, some of our "other than No" learning is also the result of making a fuss and getting what we want. As infants, we could not speak, so we used our bodies and our screams to let our parents know that we were hungry, tired, uncomfortable or even in pain. Each time we screamed, we got our parents' attention, and they usually solved our problems. It does not take long for babies to learn that lesson that when they are hungry they should simply cry and then they will be fed. This lesson is reinforced for many years, and as the child gets older there is a good chance that the lesson of the hunger cry will be applied in the form of a temper tantrum thrown by a child not getting its way. If the parents, in order to stop the tantrum, respond with exactly what the child wants, the child learns to associate that behavior with success. The "No" learning is replaced by the yes learning. The message is that throwing a tantrum will result in getting what you want.

This visit back to infancy truly does have a great deal of relevance to our work as **L.E.A.D.E.R.S.** The key lesson is that we can learn from the "no" response and even punishment, but the best learning occurs when we are rewarded for success and led with love. When our associates do something wrong, we can easily criticize them, or even punish them with negative feedback. This will obviously get the point across, but may not get them effectively trained. We are teaching them "what not to do" not the "should do" or "to do." Punishment puts the focus on what you do not want, but praise highlights what you *do* want. In short, rewards can elicit the behavior you want.

But just like the parents with a baby, we can also inadvertently reward behavior we do not want. When we allow staff to violate rules and not suffer the consequences, we are essentially telling them that the rules aren't important and it is ok to break them. If you fail to stop, counsel against or punish inappropriate behavior, it is the same as rewarding it. Reward that behavior and you will get more of it.

Great **L.E.A.D.E.R.S.** discover that the most powerful learning takes place when we reward the behavior we want. As **L.E.A.D.E.R.S.** we all must remind ourselves of this truth and act on it. The old expression, "catch your staff doing something right" is incredibly powerful. The message is clear: decide what you want, look for it, then reinforce the behavior with rewards that tell your associates what "to do" rather than saying what "not to do."

SECTION II — MINI CASE STUDY
"LATE AGAIN"

One morning about three months ago, Bill turned off his alarm without being awake and alert enough to realize that it was time to get up for work. He had been up until 3 a.m. preparing for an exam in his marketing course and he simply needed more sleep. By the time he woke up, it was 8:30 which was exactly the time he was due at work. To make matters worse, he was scheduled for a meeting at 9 with his boss.

Bill made record time getting ready, and by 9 AM he was in his car driving to the office. He got there at 9:20 and ran from his car to the conference room where the meeting was scheduled. The room was empty, which made Bill even more concerned. By the time he got to his boss's office, he was practically frantic with worry. "Ted, I am so sorry. I was up until 3 AM working on preparation for my mid-term in Marketing and this morning I turned off the alarm without realizing it."

Much to Bill's surprise, Ted was not upset and said. "I understand Bill, and we cancelled the meeting and decided to reschedule it when you were here. What time would work for you?" Bill was floored. He told Ted the best time for him and they scheduled the meeting for the afternoon.

After they rescheduled, Ted asked Bill to stay for another minute and proceeded to tell him that he had gone to school for his MBA ten years ago, and that his own experience with studying late and oversleeping made him sympathetic to Bill's situation. He even went so far as to tell Bill that he would handle some aspects of Bill's job if he had a problem in the morning again.

This morning, John slept in again because he had just finished an "all nighter" studying for a statistics course. Bill was not concerned, since he knew that Ted had allowed him to be late many times over the last several months. He felt fortunate to have Ted as a boss as it was making his work on the MBA much easier.

By the time Bill arrived in the office, he remembered that he had been expected in a meeting that had been scheduled for 7:30 this morning. Ted had made a point of reminding everybody last night, but Bill was so tired that is had completely slipped his mind. He went straight to the conference room, but the meeting was over. Ted was in his office and as soon as Bill walked in, he saw that Ted's boss, the Vice President of Sales, was there as well. Ted started the conversation with, "Bill, this being late in the morning and missing meetings has become such a serious pattern with you. The meeting this morning was to announce that my boss is leaving and that I will be taking over as the VP of sales. We were planning to announce that you and Jane would be considered for my job, but your absence made that problematic. After the meeting, we gave some more thought to the situation and I am sorry to tell you that we have decided that Jane is our candidate.

Question: Who Made The Mistake?

Well, that is actually not an easy question because both Ted and John were wrong. The sad fact is that John has a bad work habit that got even worse primarily because Ted failed to make clear what "not to do."

Ted sent a strong signal to John that is was Ok not to come to work on time. That probably was well off the mark because all Ted tried to say was, I am understanding and reasonable. Unfortunately, John learned from that first time, that Ted was flexible. As John developed the pattern with subsequent tardy behavior, Ted compounded the problem by not addressing the issue with John.

In the final analysis, the real cause of the problem is Ted. The leader is responsible for ensuring that the associates know what is expected of them as they Lead with Love™. Ted not only failed to make the expectations clear, he actually rewarded John for being late by accepting his tardiness the first time and then by subsequently failing to reprimand John when he was late again. By the time of the latest incident, Ted shows that he has ignored the failures by being willing to consider Bill for promotion.

As **L.E.A.D.E.R.S.**, we must be careful that we not only make clear what the expectations are, but also that we reward the right behavior. In this case, Ted probably failed on both points and the real loser was Bill.

SECTION III
TIPS FROM GERRY

You are probably familiar with this point, but it's a critical tip nonetheless: monetary rewards work, but praise often works better. Most of us like to be recognized, and even the most self-assured associates need to be rewarded for their positive behavior and results. Take advantage of every opportunity to acknowledge a good performance. If a staff member does something right, tell them so. If they do something truly great, then make a big deal out of the results.

On the other hand, do not reward associates out of proportion to the level of success. If all they do is to achieve the minimum that is expected, then acknowledge the achievement, but do not establish a reward that communicates delight on your part. (The exception might be when prior failures were so significant, that the success, no matter how small, is actually a break through.) If you have set a high bar for expectations, then make certain that you do not send a signal that low performance is great. If you do that, you will get low performance and your staff will never strive for the high bar. Remember, you will get the behavior you reward, so please make certain you reward what you want, not just what you get.

SECTION IV
"ASK GERRY"

Pete: I have a staff member, John, who has worked for me for three years and who has gotten an exceptional performance review each year and a salary increase to match. I just heard through the "internal grapevine" that he is quite unhappy in his current position and has been looking for another job. I must admit, I am shocked. His salary reviews have been far beyond what any other staff member has gotten. How can he possibly be unhappy?

Gerry: Pete, you have just made the mistake of thinking that a great salary increase is the only reward that matters. It does matter, if you fail to get the increase, but the increase itself is not very effective in communicating your belief that this person is a star. The performance appraisal should have sent a strong signal. Since it seems not to have done that, either you did not discuss it with him or the appraisal was not viewed as a real positive reinforcement of behavior and results. If either is the case, then you lost the opportunity to positively communicate with your staff member, and you need to take action immediately to correct that.

On the other hand, you may actually have another problem that could be even more significant. In most cases, when associates are unhappy in their jobs, they frequently are unhappy with their boss or something their boss has done or not done. I have no idea what your relationship is with John, but if there is any chance that you are falling short as a leader, then that may be the entire problem. There is no easy way to deal with this type of situation, but as you will come to understand over time, I believe that direct dialogue with the other person is usually the best approach.

I suggest that you have a chat with John and try to find out what is bothering him. I would just level with him and say, "John, I have heard that you are not completely happy in your job. My source is not important, but I really think you are doing a great job and I want to know what I can do to make you feel more comfortable. Are you willing to share with me, or to give me some thoughts on how I can make this job meet your expectations?" You may not get a straight answer, but it is in my mind worth a try. My experience is that when you openly ask people to help, they will respond by trying to be helpful.

CHAPTER 8

SELF

L.E.A.D.E.R.S. Must Lead Themselves

HOW many times have you gotten up in the morning, gone to work, returned and gone to bed not having a clue as to what you did that day? Many of us have had that happen and then passed it off as just another aspect of the daily grind. I can remember, early in my career, finding myself on such a treadmill. I was more or less adrift without any concept of where I was going.

When I took my first job, I got off to a rocket fast start. I managed to move up quickly from one job to the next, and was lucky several times to "be in the right place at the right time". My career took off, and with each new job I faced challenges of increasing intensity that took more and more time from the rest of my life. I did not complain, because I wanted to succeed. I also had the good fortune of an incredibly supportive wife who was successful and hard working on her own. She understood and shared in my desire for success. All of this fed a frenzy of activity, most of which I thought was good.

To be honest, I had no real idea where all of this work was leading me. I had spent virtually no time thinking through what I was doing in my career or where my career was going. As long as I was moving forward, with more and more challenges and responsibilities, there was no time or reason to think about me. I was consumed by the job, and for a very long time that was all that I needed.

After I had worked for about eight years, it finally dawned on me that I was doing nearly the same things that I had been doing at the start of my career. Yes, I was working in bigger organizations, had a bigger title and was making more money; but in many ways, what I had done in the past year was the same as what I had in the previous eight years. This realization was shocking, but also life-altering.

For the first time I realized that I was not in a "career", I was in a job; and that I was not necessarily doing what I wanted rather, I was doing what my boss needed and wanted me to do. Satisfying the needs and wants of a boss is not in itself a bad thing. On the contrary, being the "go-to-person" has a great deal of merit, as was evidenced by my explosive rise in the hierarchy. The problem was that I was paying no regard to my needs, my career, and my future. That was when I started to focus on "Self."

Making my "self" a priority does not mean being selfish. I didn't reduce my efforts at work, or avoid the hard assignments; but I started to ask myself the "what about me?" kind of questions. Those questions lead to the conclusion that I needed to make some changes to achieve the vision I had for my future. In short, I started thinking about the last letter in our **L.E.A.D.E.R.S.** mnemonic, only now it had a priority in my life.

As I said earlier, making myself a priority was not "selfish". The distinction here is that the self-focused person looks beyond what "is" and envisions what can and will be. This was the time when I really started to ask the question, "How am I doing?" Although I had given and received many performance reviews over the years, I had never before thought to do one for myself.

The short version of the story is that I did my review and then spent a great deal of time deciding what I wanted to be at some time in the future. This process triggered a series of actions on my part, through which I was ultimately transformed into a very different person. I went back to school and took a large number of courses that would enhance my knowledge, skills and behaviors. I started focusing on outside activities that would establish my credibility in areas I needed to add to my portfolio. I read new and different books, attended new organizational meetings, joined some new service and professional clubs, and I networked in all of them. In essence, I remade myself. At the end of about five years, I had the experience, credentials and contacts to be considered for a much different set of jobs. It took some time, but I got my career on the track that I wanted and I never looked back.

By applying the leadership skills embodied in the word L.E.A.D.E.R.S., I lead myself to a new and fulfilling career. You can, and must, do your own review of where you are, where you're headed, and where it is that you really want to be. Take the time to consider *your* SELF and lead yourself with love!

SECTION II — MINI CASE STUDY
"I QUIT !"

Brent had been a supervisor at the same organization for eleven years. As the company's expert in automobile financing, he knew that he was respected for his expertise. Although he enjoyed that recognition, he felt unfulfilled in his job.

At home in the evening and on weekends, Brent would spend hours drawing and painting. He had discovered several years ago that he was a pretty good artist, and that it gave him great pleasure to create a painting that people would admire and enjoy. He wished that he could spend more time painting, but there were only so many hours left in the day after work.

Today, Brent went to work and something snapped. He realized that he was 38 years old and that he simply did not like his job. He liked the people, he liked the company, but his work just felt like a drain. Right after lunch, Brent went to his boss and quit. His boss was shocked, and frankly so was Brent.

What's In Store for Brent ?

Brent probably did the right thing, but at the wrong time. He acted on impulse, and now will be facing no income and no plan for the future. If you are feeling like Brent, unfulfilled and drained by your job, please step back and give yourself a chance think the situation through and make plans. Becoming somebody or something else is a process, and it requires not only following your heart, but also creating a plan for the journey.

The first step is to love yourself. You should care enough to invest the time in thinking through where you want to be, and how to get there. Perhaps Brent has decided that painting is important to him and that it's what he wants to do. The problem is that the expression "starving artist" is not just an expression-- for many it is a reality. Brent is only focusing on his desire to paint, when what he needs to do is step back and rationally asses how he can fulfill all of his dreams and aspirations. With his artistic talent, it is possible that a career change to the advertising department in his current company might be a more practical solution while also fulfilling his outlet for creativity.

Maybe Brent should take a painting class to see just how much better he can get. If he has extraordinary talent, formal training could enable him to truly make a living from his art. Another option would be to stay with his current job and try selling his paintings "on the side." It could be that although painting is a great therapy for him, it is not something he should be doing full time. On the other hand, if he can become commercially successful, there will be plenty of time to shift his life in that direction.

I am not suggesting that Brent should stay in his job and remain miserable forever. He should consider his short- and long-term options, and develop a plan that will lead to where he really wants to be. Just walking away from that which he knows, and has been very good at, could be a disaster. Making the *right* move, not just *some* move, is what he--and you--should always aim to do.

SECTION III
TIPS FROM GERRY

Caring for the self is often precipitated (as in my case) by a realization that something is wrong with the status quo. Initially, the focus is on what's wrong. Ideally, you should start with a clear understanding of what you are doing, then assess what it is that is wrong, and finally, what courses of action might be available to you.

Being unhappy in a job does not always result from being in the wrong job; it often results from doing a job for the wrong person or in the wrong organization. If that is your case, explore all of the options, including a candid discussion with your boss. Many times, those conversations can spare you from making a radical move by dealing with the issue directly and effectively. Bosses often have no idea that they are in some respect problematic for the people working for them. A careful, but honest discussion can help clear the air and enable you and your boss to focus on improving the relationship.

At other times, a discussion that brings to light a discomfort with a job can lead to a quality reassignment, either within the same section or department, or elsewhere within the same firm. I have not met many leaders who wanted to make their staff miserable. Most of us actually do know how to love; but even if your boss has not learned that core concept, he or she probably cares enough to try to help relieve your pain. Always give your boss the benefit of the doubt, and I think you will be pleasantly surprised.

SECTION IV
"ASK GERRY"

Phil: I love my job, but I am getting nowhere in pay. What can I do?

Gerry: This is a short and simple question, regarding a complex issue that can rarely be resolved with a short and simple answer. On the one hand, you should consider yourself extremely fortunate that you love your job. On the other hand, you feel unfortunate in your pay. That could be a real problem, or a real *perception* problem.

While not everyone loves their job, most people are convinced that they don't make enough money. The question is whether you are being underpaid for your job, or if you are in a job that just doesn't pay well. For example, teachers often love their job; yet many of them leave teaching because they cannot make the money that they want. Although they may well deserve to earn more, teachers are paid according to a general salary range for that profession. The same is true for every job in every industry. This is not an economics lesson, but it is important to remember that the "laws of supply and demand" tend to set the value a society puts on workers. Many people in teaching love what they do, and do it in spite of the fact that they are not the highest paid people in their neighborhood.

On the other hand, if you are actually underpaid for the job you are doing, then you may have a problem that needs action. The first option is always to have that conversation with your boss. If that seems impossible, then maybe you need to "test the market" outside your company.

The other factor could be that your performance is not up to "Expectations." If not, and assuming you know if it is or not, then you need to work on your "self" to find a way to improve. If that is the case, your commitment to self will drive you to either get better trained, better focused on the key skills and knowledge necessary to get better, or you will ask the company to help. All of these are things you need to take ownership of. Do that, and you will have explored the possible alternative futures.

Do not stay in your current job if the pay is a problem that you simply cannot get out of your head. If you do, you will eventually become bitter and angry and then your performance will deteriorate and the pay situation will probably get worse.

Zach: I'm lost at my job. I hate my boss, I hate the work I do and I have been living with these feelings for the past four years. What can I do?

Gerry: Zach, I feel sorry for you. That is a sad tale, and one that I hear much too often when I talk to leaders. My first answer is: you must set out to change your job. That may mean that you need to "change jobs" entirely or, it may be that you need to change things about your current job. Whatever the case, I absolutely advise you to do one of those two things, immediately. There are scores of reasons why we dislike our work. Some are our fault and frankly, some are the organization's fault. The most important thing you need to do is to honestly determine all of the reasons why you do not like your job. Sit down and honestly evaluate yourself and your expectations and determine precisely where things went wrong and pinpoint what they are. I unfortunately cannot answer that for you, but I can tell you that once you have come to your own conclusions, you need to do something to eliminate that pain you are feeling. In fact, once you sort through the questions that I have asked of you, I hope you that will write again so we can work together on the ways in which you can move forward towards a positive work experience.

CHAPTER 9
L.E.A.D.E.R.S.

THE JOURNEY FROM LOVE TO SELF

O ur journey began with understanding of the role of *love* in leadership. Love initially sets the tone of the relationship with your associates and then love concludes with a focus on creating a positive self-concept and being a leader for yourself. By committing to honing on your capacity to love your associates and committing to the role of loving and leading yourself, you must then: set personal expectations, establish correct assignments, focus on the development, provide effective evaluations, and deliver timely rewards. These leadership practices are necessary to foster, encourage, and assure peak performance from your associates however, the real intensity of your efforts must be on yourself.

The role of a "leader" places a burden on you that cannot be treated lightly. When you were an individual performer, your capacity to deliver results was the true measure of your success. As a leader you will probably continue to participate in tasks that generate results for your organization, but your true measure of success shifts dramatically. You must help your associates achieve success as individuals and as a team.

You must not allow the term **L.E.A.D.E.R.S.** confuse you. You are not leading the work; you are leading the workers.

Your role is entirely new since now you must get your greatest happiness from the success of others rather than from your own. This is not a selfless act. It is quite self-focused. As a leader, your only avenue to success is for your unit to succeed. Having a staff to lead means that the organization believes more than one associate is required to achieve the unit goals; hence you alone cannot achieve success. Your staff's pain of failure or excitement at success must be yours. Your goal must be to help staff members stay focused on the goals, because their achievements will be your achievement.

The most effective way for your associates to grow and succeed is to learn from you. Once you are the leader, you are the guiding light. You must be a bright beacon guiding them to achieve. Unfortunately, most of us are not ready for that role and responsibility. Few of us ask for it. Being the appointed leader usually comes to us because we were good at doing the work, not because we were groomed to lead.

We have focused on the key principles required of effective **L.E.A.D.E.R.S.** I have tried to emphasize the simplicity of the concepts, but the actual tasks of leading are tough work. Just as you needed to be trained to do your previous work assignment as an individual performer, so must you be given the boost required to develop the skills of a leader. There are few shortcuts to this development, and although most organizations recognize the challenge, few have discovered the secret of developing peak performance work leaders. All too often, **L.E.A.D.E.R.S.** are "thrown into the water" to sink or swim with no real swimming lessons. Most **L.E.A.D.E.R.S.** tend to "doggy paddle" their way to survival, but many never learn to swim. They simply learn to avoid drowning. Are you one of those?

Just as in the case of a child, the only rational way to learn how to swim is to be taught by a person who has the knowledge and skills. The best way to learn how to lead is to work for a great leader, but if you are one who has been left to "sink or swim," I recommend you take action immediately. Find a great leader, and then find a way to get into that unit. The payback will be enormous. Armed with the 7 key **L.E.A.D.E.R.S.** principles, you will have the knowledge to develop the skills and attitudes you will need to learn to swim.

You need to become the great leader that all associates want to work for. When that happens, you will have made the transition from manager to leader.

And, just as importantly, once you have gained the skills required to be a great leader it will then be your turn to pass on your knowledge, skills, and attitudes to your associates. The reason is simple: somebody in your unit will probably some day be asked to step into your shoes as leader and one of those associates is probably working for you because he or she wants to learn from a great leader. Because you love them all, you owe it to all your associates to help your successor be more ready than you were.

CONTINUE YOUR LEARNING!

If you have enjoyed the insights from this book, then you will greatly benefit from reading my book, *You're In Charge...What Now?* As I mentioned previously, that book provided the foundation and is the premise by which this book was written. *You're In Charge...What Now?* is designed to help **L.E.A.D.E.R.S.** at every level, become better at leading the people they are responsible to and for. It is loaded with additional practical insights, just like I have tried to do here. ..

You're In Charge...What Now? is available to purchase on our website www.deltennium.com or www.leadwithlove.com and it is available in soft cover, CD/ audio-book format and in an abbreviated flash-card format called MemCards.

Consider the comments from some top leaders in a variety of industries regarding my book.

You're In Charge...What Now? Book Reviews

"Managers are a dime a dozen, but leaders are priceless. Teaching principles as solid as setting expectations, and as radical as understanding love, Gerald M. Czarnecki's seven steps put the new leader's focus where it belongs--on finding, developing, and rewarding teams of outstanding performers. Any manager aspiring to leadership would be wise to study Gerald's advice."

Jeff Taylor, Founder and Chairman, Monster.com

"Recently appointed to your first position leading others? This book is for you! It describes in concrete detail exactly what it takes to get those actually doing the work of the organization to perform at exceptional levels. Powerful, accurate and, most importantly, eminently useable, Czarnecki's insights provide a concrete blueprint for managerial success."

Jerry I. Porras, Lane Professor of Organizational Behavior and Change, Emeritus, Graduate School of Business, Stanford University and Co-author of "Built to Last"

"If you are a working leader, and you want to get things done, this book is for you. This book is full of practical insights and tips to make you a more effective leader."

Ram Charan, Consultant to CEOs and Board of Directors and Co-author of "Execution"

"You're in Charge..." is outstanding reading for first time managers as they strive to expand their leadership capacity. Gerry Czarnecki distilled his years

of experience at all levels of an organization into an easy-to-read, pragmatic primer on making the transition from supervisor to leader."

Edward B. Rust Jr., Chairman & CEO,
State Farm Insurance Companies

"I loved this book. The concept of "work leaders" is the most compelling and effective approach to blending the role of managers and leaders. It is a practical, comprehensive approach that can truly help "work leaders" be successful in every organization."

Rhoda Olsen, President & Chief Operating Officer,
Great Clips, Inc.

"You're in Charge... What Now?" is a perfect textbook for a "rookie manager." The seven essential steps for Work Leaders Success are nicely organized to facilitate the learning process. Each Chapter has Tips to guide the learner, and each chapter ends in a case study with thought provoking questions. I could easily see this book being used to augment management training — with weekly reading assignments followed by group discussion."

Gary Davis, Executive Vice President, Chief Human Resources and
Administration Officer, J.C. Penney Company, Inc.

OTHER MANAGEMENT TRAINING/
SPEAKING SERVICES

While my thoughts here are an expression of my personal thoughts and advice on becoming a better leader, I do not work alone in providing resources, support and guidance to leaders on all levels. The Deltennium Group is an alliance of speakers, trainers, coaches and consultants with diverse professional backgrounds and areas of expertise that make us uniquely capable to assist all variety of leaders and organizations. We are committed to engaging, energizing, training, and facilitating the development of organizational and individual excellence through effective strategy and leadership.

Deltennium offers a range of programs that can be used to train everyone from first-level sales managers to top-level boards of directors. Every individual and organization faces unique challenges, and Deltennium works accordingly. My associates and I are flexible and adapt our speaking, training, coaching and consulting engagements to meet the needs of the individual or organization. The goal is success, and whether it's the aid of a book, seminar, coach or consultant that you need to achieve it, you'll find that Deltennium can help.

Sample Seminar & Keynote Topics

- You're In Charge...
  What Now?
- Aloha Leadership
- Nature, Nurture, Choice
  and Chance
- How To Get Fired By Doing
  A Great Job!
- Board Development
  programs

Other Areas of Leadership and Management Focus

- Corporate Governance
- Work Leader Success
- Career Planning and the Keys
  to Success
- Coping With Change
- Self Renewal

For more information on our seminars and products, please visit our website:

http://www.deltennium.com

Or contact us directly at:
Director of Marketing & Human Resources
Robyn Lighthammer
6830 Elm Street, Suite 5
McLean, VA 22101
703 992-5432

light.hammer@verizon.net

Gerry has written three books:
You're In Charge... What Now?,
You're a Non-Profit Director... What Now?
and *Success Principles For Leaders*.
He has a fourth book being published in the Spring of 2009
which will be entitled *Lead With Love*™.

QUICK ORDER FORM

20% off Retail Price

📞 Telephone orders to: 703 992-5432

 Email orders to: light.hammer@verizon.net

📄 Fax orders to: 703 842-8773

www Order Online at :   www.deltennium.com

 Mail Orders to: The Deltennium Group, Inc.
6830 Elm Street, Suite #5 McLean, VA 22101

Quantity	Title	Retail	Discount	
	You're In Charge...What Now?	Softcover Book	~~$17.95~~	$14.36
	You're In Charge...What Now?	6 CD/Audio	~~$69.50~~	$55.60
	You're In Charge...What Now?	Mem Cards	~~$9.95~~	$7.96
	You're A Non-Profit Director... What Now?	Book	~~$14.95~~	$7.96
	Success Principles for Leaders	Book	~~$14.95~~	$7.96

US Shipping: $4.00 for the first item and $2.00 for each additional item.

With larger quantity orders, discounts will apply so please call for an estimate!

Name:_____

Company:_____

Address:_____

City:_____State:_____Zip:_____

Telephone:_____

Email Address:_____

QUICK ORDER FORM

20% off Retail Price

 Telephone orders to: 703 992-5432

 Email orders to: light.hammer@verizon.net

 Fax orders to: 703 842-8773

www Order Online at :   www.deltennium.com

✉ Mail Orders to: The Deltennium Group, Inc.
6830 Elm Street, Suite #5 McLean, VA 22101

Quantity	Title	Retail	Discount	
	You're In Charge...What Now?	Softcover Book	~~$17.95~~	$14.36
	You're In Charge...What Now?	6 CD/Audio	~~$69.50~~	$55.60
	You're In Charge...What Now?	Mem Cards	~~$9.95~~	$7.96
	You're A Non-Profit Director... What Now?	Book	~~$14.95~~	$7.96
	Success Principles for Leaders	Book	~~$14.95~~	$7.96

US Shipping: $4.00 for the first item and $2.00 for each additional item.

With larger quantity orders, discounts will apply so please call for an estimate!

Name:_____

Company:_____

Address:_____

City:_____State:_____Zip:_____

Telephone:_____

Email Address:_____

ABOUT THE AUTHOR

Gerald Czarnecki is the Chairman & CEO of The Deltennium Group, Inc., a consulting group which helps individuals and organizations achieve peak performance through: effective leadership, board governance, focused strategy and sound financial management. He also serves as President & CEO of O2Media, Inc., an organization providing world class television production and programming.

In 1993, Gerry was recruited by Louis Gerstner of IBM to serve as Senior Vice President where he had worldwide responsibility for Human Resources, Real Estate, Quality Programs, nonmanufacturing procurement and aviation. Prior to joining IBM, he had held a number of Executive level positions in the Banking and Financial Services industry including serving as CEO of both publicly and privately held banks, one which was owned by an investor group headed by former Secretary of the Treasury, William Simon.

He holds a B.S. in Economics from Temple University, a M.A. in Economics from Michigan State University, is a CPA and has a Doctor of Humane Letters from National University. He is a member of the board of directors of State Farm Insurance where he serves as Chair of the Audit Committee; State Farm Bank; State Farm Fire & Casualty and Del Global Technology, where he serves as Chair of the Audit Committee. He also serves on several Non-Profit boards: National University where he is Chairman of The Board; The National Leadership Institute; NACD Florida where he serves as Chairman of the Board; Private Capital, Inc.; Junior Achievement Worldwide, Inc, where he serves on the Board of Governors, Chairman of the HR, Compensation Committee and Pension Committees and recently served for almost one year as their Interim President & CEO.